Nonprofit Strategic Planning

By

Shea Smith III

SHEA SMITH III

CONTENTS

ACKNOWLEDGMENTS

This book is an update and redraft of the original book of the same title that was self-published in 1997. The author thanks Nancy Shohet West for help in editorial support and managing its printing, Kristine Zards Rencs for cover design, and Elaine Sidzik for solving some computer problems encountered in creating the new document from the old.

PREFACE

The purpose of this book is to provide the know-how for leading a nonprofit agency (NPs) through the planning process **with minimum wasted effort**; the end result, a written plan that clearly points out the key issues facing the agency, and how it will handle them.

All organizations – both profit-making organizations (FPs) as well as nonprofits (NPs) – have three basic employee levels:

> (1) Top Echelons
>
> (2) Departments/Divisions
>
> (3) Staff

And there are two basic kinds of planning:

> (1) Top-down planning
>
> (2) Bottom-up planning

Top-down planning is where the top echelon develops the plan for the organization and then asks the departments and divisions and possibly other stakeholders to critique it.

Bottom-up planning is where the top echelon asks the departments and divisions to submit plans for their operations accompanied by guidelines, formats, deadlines, and assumptions upon which the plans are to be based. The top echelon then consolidates the departmental/divisional plans into a total enterprise plan.

Bottom-up is usually the choice of large organizations, top-down by smaller ones – hence the most common choice of NPs.

Writing the Plan

The author has experimented with different formats over several decades and has settled on the following:

1. The Situation

2. Mission/Vision

3. External Environment

   a. Threats

   b. Opportunities

4. Internal Environment

   a. Strengths

   b. Weaknesses

5. Key Issues

6. Strategies & Goals

7. Financial Projections

8. Planning Control

9. Governance

Each of the above will be dealt with in separate chapters. Each chapter will describe what the subject heading should accomplish and give examples of how to write it.

How to Carry Out the Process?

A strategic planning committee is needed to carry out the process and keep it up to date. The chair can be a consultant or insider, preferably the latter if one already exists with proper qualifications.

The chairperson and CEO need to agree upon the following:

- The outline for the process and the sequence.
- Who should be members of the committee.
- Who should be the primary writer of the plan.
- How the meetings will be run:
    - Use of Roberts Rules of Order if size of the committee justifies that formality.
    - Starting on time and limiting duration; 1½ - 2 hours is a practical limit.
- Appoint a secretary to take minutes and provide drafts of the plan as it is developed; distribute redrafts to committee members after each meeting.

When To Begin Writing?

Writing should begin before the first meeting with drafts of The Situation and Mission/Vision provided by the secretary.

Initial drafts will always be very rough. Even so, meetings will be more productive if the attendees have something in writing to which they can react. Redrafts should be written after each meeting; later sections should be added as they are developed; a new draft thus far agreed upon should then be distributed to the planning committee before the next meeting. Continue this process up to the final draft.

Planning Committee

The right people and the right size can make the difference between a good experience and a bad one. Who are the right people? Certainly, those who will be most responsible for implementation of the plan. The committee should definitely include:

- The Chair of the Planning Committee
- The CEO
- The Chief Financial Officer

Others to consider are the chairman of the board, development director, other board members and/or staff members who have demonstrated strong interest, good judgment, and conceptual thinking capability. One or two clients of the agency might also be considered.

Six is an ideal number, but not a sacred number. Much depends upon the quality and personalities of the group. Numbers beyond six tend to slow up the process. But one bad appointment to the committee can slow up progress much more than size.

Time Horizons

How far in the future long-range strategic plans should be projected will vary with circumstances. If the agency is facing a financial crisis a year or less may be appropriate; certainly, if the crisis may mean the end of the agency, there is little point in pursuing plans covering several years.

The situation will not often be this critical and the time horizon should be more than one year. But how many? This depends upon how stable are the external and internal environments and the kind of business in which the agency is engaged.

In manufacturing businesses, ten years may elapse between the time a new plant is proposed and the time it is operational. Hence, an agency that makes products by handicapped people might need a ten year horizon for its planning.

From our experience, however, we would say that ten years is a limit, and, in most cases, three to six years is sufficient.

Who Writes Plan?

The agency should be responsible for the final draft of the plan, not a consultant. It is important that the agency feels that it is *their* plan and not a plan recommended by an outsider.

But what often happens is this. The Planning Committee has been appointed; it has agreed to the outline to be used for the long range plan; someone has been selected to take minutes and be responsible for writing drafts of the plan. Still, after two or three meetings, little progress is made in writing drafts of the plan in the agreed upon format. At this point, time can be saved by the consultant coming to the rescue and writing a first draft.

After the first draft has been written and discussed, responsibility for incorporating revisions and additions recommended by the planning committee should then become the responsibility of the designated insider on the committee.

This insider could be the board member who is chairman of the planning committee of the Board, the executive director/president, or any other insider who has the necessary writing skill.

Who Chairs Meetings?

The lead consultant would normally be the best chair of the planning sessions. This assumes that one or two consultants have been recruited to take an active part in the process, not used simply as a sounding board.

The consultant would have had lots of experience at running such sessions and thereby be able to guide the discussions and procedures to accomplish the effort with minimum wasted motion.

Whoever is chairperson, however, should not be expected to both chair the meetings as well as take minutes. The executive director of the agency should designate one of the insiders on the planning committee to be secretary of the sessions.

How Much Time?

How much time should it take to write a long-range plan? A half-dozen meetings over a six to nine month period would normally be sufficient for most agencies. This assumes that the agency does not already have a plan; if it does, less time may be needed.

More than six to nine months might be required if the agency is large and has many complicated problems or if some research is needed before a plan can be written.

Quality of the people working on the plan and how much homework they do between meetings is the determinant.

Two Versions or One?

The final draft may be in two versions: one highly confidential for use only by the top echelon of the organization; the other for the public and lower echelons. Usually the confidential report is produced first. Deletion of confidential parts of the plan provide the other version.

An **extremely condensed write-up** of the LRP is also a possibility — one, for instance, that covers both sides of an 8 1/2 x 11 inch piece of paper, in columnar style so that it can be folded to make an

8 1/2 x 3 2/3 inch pamphlet, easily carried in an inside jacket pocket. Such a version can be highly useful in providing very broad distribution to existing and potential stakeholders.

Why different versions? The long range plan can be an important instrument for raising money. It helps to provide confidence that money donated toward accomplishment of the agency's mission will be well spent.

Different versions of the plan, therefore, written specifically for different audiences, are often worthwhile.

Review/Revise

Parts of any plan may become out of date soon after it is written because of an unanticipated turn of events. This does not mean that a strategic plan should be rewritten several times a year. It does suggest, however, that at least once a year it should be reviewed and brought up to date.

Sometimes a new development will be so important that it invalidates large segments of a plan. When this happens, the strategic plan should be revised at once unless a contingency plan already exists in anticipation of the event.

Conclusion

Properly managed, developing a strategic plan can be fun and a very rewarding experience. The major ingredients are:

1. The right process.

2. The right people.

3. The right number of people.

4. The right homework between meetings.

5. The right concentration on issues – key, not all.

6. The right involvement of stakeholders.

CHAPTER ONE

The Situation

A succinct write-up of the present situation sets the stage, provides the backdrop for the planning effort. This section establishes the raison d'etre for the task. It is designed to put everyone involved on the same level of understanding of why the effort is being made at this time.

The situation statement will have some overlap with later sections — particularly key issues. Overlap is inevitable because the peculiar circumstances which prompts writing or rewriting a long range plan is almost always the result of a few key issues.

Seldom, however, does the situation write-up cover *all* key issues, nor should it. When the situation statement is first written, the external and internal environments have not yet been analyzed; therefore not all key issues shall likely have surfaced. It simply identifies the *major* key issue(s) that prompted writing the plan. It does not identify them all; that comes later.

There is no standard format for this section. Some situation write-ups are quite brief; others, because of circumstances, can be long and detailed. Here are three case histories.

Case History #1 — A School for the Handicapped

The Special School for Children has been in operation for 47 years. Classes were initially held in a church, but in 1970 the school moved to a building on the grounds of a college campus. Sale of school campus property in 1980 forced the school to move in that year to its present location in a building vacated by a local school district. The School is non-denominational.

The present facility is an improvement over the former location. The move, however, has substantially increased operating costs requiring both an increase in tuition and more than a doubling of the need for fund raising. The net result has been a serious weakening of the School's finances.

The School appears to have filled a niche in the network of services available to developmentally disabled children of the community. Continuing to operate the school is judged by the Board to be worthwhile. The major issue is "how to put the School back on a sound financial footing."

Case History #2 - Help for the Blind

Help for the Blind (HFB) for several years has felt the need for better facilities. Renovation of the current facility or building a new one is under consideration.

In 1985 Turner Construction Company studied how best to provide facilities that would be needed for the long term. Their conclusion was that it would be cheaper and less disruptive to build an entirely new facility rather than try to renovate the present one.

A study was made by a firm specializing in fund raising, to assess the feasibility of a capital fund-raising campaign of $6 million to carry out the building program. The first step would be development of a strategic plan as marketing tool to sell its feasibility.

Case History #3 - A Mental Health Agency

A mental health agency was experiencing major change in both the external and internal environment.

The Center was changed three years ago as a separate free-standing administrative agent of the state Department of Mental Health (DMH) to provide community-based services for residents and homeless of one of the cities in the state.

The change was made as a result of a shift in DMH philosophy. Prior to the Center's inception, patients were served by two mental hospitals, most often through the Emergency Room. There was no attempt to follow a patient's history and progress.

When the Center was established every patient was assigned a case manager who could purchase services from an array of psychiatrists, therapists, and day programs. A case manager facilitated point-of-entry to services and followed a client through to discharge. This change required training staff to assume new roles and to establish contracts with private providers of services. It also required complete reorganization: bringing together the staffs of the two mental hospitals, decreasing the number of direct care staff, and increasing the number of staff to carry out the case manager function.

Six months after the Center was established, it became a certified Community Psychiatric Rehabilitation Center (CPRC). This provided the Center with a new financial resource by allowing it to have much of its state funding matched by Medicaid. It also meant that instead of just being a "broker" of services, the Center itself could become an active supplier of services.

During this transition period, budget cuts at the state level forced the closing of one of the two state hospitals and the downsizing of the other. Responsibility for handling the gap in services caused by these actions was assigned to the Center.

These changes put a tremendous strain on the management, staff, and physical facilities of the Center. Lots of progress was made, but lingering problems included: (1) lack of complete control of persons entering the system; (2) a 3-month waiting list for services; (3) lack of information for evaluating and prioritizing the needs of clients.

The Center decided to incorporate the planning process into its management system to handle these problems and others that would surface in the future.

Planning Philosophy

Sometimes agencies like to preamble The Situation with a statement of their planning philosophy — its purpose, the process, and the thinking behind the process. Here are two examples:

1. The long range plan when developed will provide a framework for directing the agency's resources in a cost-effective way to achieve its goals and objectives. It will focus efforts on those opportunities and problems which are paramount to its staff and clients, and the community. The plan will provide a mechanism for measuring realization of its goals by periodically evaluating progress.

   It must be realistic in its achievability and flexible in responding to a changing environment. Because of inevitable changes in both the external and internal environments the plan will be revised at least annually and more often if needed. At all times, it will be consistent with the agency's by-laws and policies. An edited version of the plan will be written to provide an effective sales tool in fundraising programs.

2. Here is another, taken from the mental health center mentioned earlier:

This plan was developed to address the multiple changes and risks that the Center faces in developing a comprehensive system of services for persons with serious psychiatric disabilities who reside in the city or are homeless. The plan is designed to:

1) Identify the key needs of current and future customers and the key issues the Center faces in satisfying these needs.

2) Present a vision of a comprehensive system of services based upon a shared philosophy of mission and approach to service delivery.

3) Specify strategies, goals, and actions to effectively manage the process and measure performance as the service delivery system evolves.

4) Develop mechanisms for making the best possible use of existing resources and obtain additional resources to accomplish the Center's mission.

The planning process includes extensive input from consumers, families, staff, providers of services, and the community at large. Steps to be taken are the following:

1) A two-day retreat of staff. Staff input to philosophy and mission was considered critical as service delivery is dependent upon every staff member's contribution. They are the true implementers of the plan set forth.

2) Multiple meetings with three volunteer consultants for input, review, and critique of the plan as well as the planning process.

3) Extensive review of the State's Mental Health Plan.

4) Multiple meetings with staff following the two-day retreat to keep them informed and involved in the planning process.

5) A comprehensive customer needs assessment developed and conducted by a professional market researcher.

6) Formal and informal meetings and discussions with service providers, consumers, and key community agencies.

7) Extensive input, review, and prioritization and support from the agency's Advisory Board.

CHAPTER TWO

MISSION/VISION

The mission statement for nonprofit organizations states the vision for achieving a unique niche in society in sufficient detail to clearly indicate its parameters of operation and the principals to be followed in reaching its ultimate destination.

Medtronic, an FP producer of implantable biomedical devices, is an impressive example. Between 1979 and 2001 per share stock value increased at a compound growth rate of almost 30%. Most of that growth took place during the decade, 1991-2001, when the company had hired a very gifted new CEO. One of the first things he did when he joined the company was to restate the company's mission.

Instead of a mission to achieve a level of financial success, as was prevalent by many FPs in those days, he decided that Medtronic's principal mission should be to restore people's quality of life and health. He probably thought if we do that well, everything else, including financial success, will happen; and it did.

Sometimes **vision** is considered to be something different from **mission**. Is there a difference or are they the same? Their concept is so similar that separately written mission and vision statements invariably overlap. To avoid this problem, we recommend explaining that your use of the word **Mission** also includes **Vision**.

The major purposes of mission statements are:

1. To imbue the entire organization with a sense of mission so that it will constantly strive for its fulfillment.

2. To project the kind of image the institution wishes to have with its stakeholders.

3. To provide a marketing tool for raising money.

The mission statement provides the foundation for strategies and tactics; any decision on plans and actions must stand the test of questioning: "Are they compatible with the mission?"

Missions of NPs

Let's look at a few mission statements for NPs. Here is one from a school for the handicapped:

Long Cross School's (LCS) principal mission is to maximize the development of disabled and delayed children from ages two to ten by providing the opportunities for them to realize their fullest potential. All disabilities, except autistic, physical handicaps requiring physical therapy, and psychiatric problems, come within its province; LCS will particularly strive to serve the multi-handicapped child.

The School operates in the metropolitan Chicago area and will continue to do so. Number of students is 50 maximum. Speech and language development, occupational therapy, and special education classroom are, and will continue to be, the principal thrusts of the school.

LCS's role in the community is to provide services some of which are not offered by area school districts and to provide a private school alternative for families with disabled children. LCS will work with other schools, agencies, and professionals as appropriate to pursue the best interests of the children and their families.

Note how well this statement describes the parameters of its operations — what disabilities it does include as well as those that are not included.

Here is another from an agency that provides employment for the blind.

The purpose of HFB (Help For the Blind) is to assist legally blind people increase their employment opportunities, independence, and integration into society.

HFB employs blind workers while simultaneously improving production efficiencies so as to maximize operating profit. Operating profit is reinvested to grow the business so that the blind work force can increase.

As a service organization, HFB is committed to promoting employment opportunity, integration and independence for its own blind and legally blind employees and others in the community by developing/supporting programs which address these needs.

Here is a final example of a mission statement from a mental health agency:

Our mission is to maximize the independence, productivity, and quality of life of persons with serious psychiatric disabilities through community based services and supports that are:

- Accessible — readily available when and where needed.
- Individualized — designed to meet the unique needs of each individual.
- Rehabilitative — facilitates and maximizes the process of   "recovery."

Our **management philosophy** is that the system should be based upon the following principles:

- Services that are flexible and adaptable.
- Persons with psychiatric disabilities have basic human needs: aspirations, rights, privileges, opportunities, and responsibilities like all other citizens in our community.
- Quality of life is an inherent goal of all persons including those with mental illness.
- Community resources are of utmost importance in enhancing quality of life.

- The rights, wishes, and needs of the mentally disabled are paramount in planning and delivering mental health services.
- The ideal service system should be accessible, compassionate, empathetic, sensitive, informed, and account- able to those it serves.
- Staff well-being and quality of life in the work environment promotes effective service delivery.
- Research and evaluation followed up by subsequent training are primary tools to provide the knowledge and skill base required to operate effectively.

Our **code of conduct** includes:

- Primary focus on customer satisfaction.
- Planning approach based upon needs assessment of our customer groups.
- Provide an environment that will attract the finest cadre of people and programs, challenge their talents, and empower them to be creative.
- Give staff and outside service groups the opportunity to participate in developing strategies for improving the system.

- Develop and adhere to mechanisms that will make us accountable to the people we serve.
- Fully use the private and public mental health resources available within the community.
- Continuously refine our system to improve quality and eliminate duplication through ongoing evaluation, research, and training.
- Provide a physical environment and open door policy that will facilitate effective communication.

CONCLUSION

Mission/Vision statements are important; and the trend seems to be in the direction of greater-and-greater recognition of their importance. They have become a management tool to keep the organization striving to achieve superior performance in the field(s) of its choice; moreover, to instill **enthusiasm** throughout the organization in the process.

They are not easy to write. They require deep insight and consensus on where the NP has been and where, long term, it wishes to go. They tend to be long-lasting — not subject to frequent change.

CHAPTER THREE

EXTERNAL ENVIRONMENT

Up to this point you have described the significant facets of your present situation and stated your mission and vision of your ultimate destination in society. The next step is to analyze the two major forces that impact upon an institution's planning — the external environment and the internal environment. Both are prime determinants of key issues.

The internal environment is stated in terms of strengths (S) and weaknesses (W); the external environment, in terms of opportunities (O) and threats (T). They together are often referred to as **SWOT Analysis.** They change constantly.

Six areas make up the external environment:

    1. The Economy

    2. Government

    3. Advocacy and special interest groups

    4. Sociological Factors

    5. Competition

    6. Technology

1. The Economy

During recessions, private education will see a shift toward public education. Child care will be affected by employment as well as by the ability to pay for the service. The need for family services will grow as a result of the tensions that poor economic conditions create in families. Demand for services for the destitute will grow. Demand for products produced by the handicapped may decline. These are but a few examples among many.

Most important for NPs is the effect that economic conditions have upon fund raising. Donations by private individuals will decline sharply in recession periods. Corporate giving will decline some, but usually not as much; corporations usually create foundations for giving money away for the purpose of maintaining a steady flow of funds for worthwhile causes regardless of economic conditions.

2. Government

Federal funding of societal issues often has major impact on NPs. So do aberrations in the purchase of goods and services. For example, the Adoption Assistance and Child Welfare Act became law in 1980; although this law was never effectively implemented at the Federal level, several states enacted similar laws many of which have been beneficial to family preservation and reducing the number of children assigned to foster parents.

For agencies that provide employment for the handicapped, the Wagner-O'Day Act of 1938 was a great benefit. It established the policy of government procurement of goods produced by the blind and severely handicapped — goods that are of equal quality and price to what is available from private industry.

The creation of Special School Districts have impacted private institutions for the education of handicapped children. And the ever-changing policies and funding of these Districts continue to create instability for these private schools.

Another example is The Education for All Handicapped Children Act. This Act provides for education programs for handicapped children; it involves testing programs to help insure that education programs for children are appropriate; financially, it assists state and local governments to provide the programs. The Act has had major impact on agencies involved with handicapped children, such as the Learning Disabilities Association.

When a new federal health care program is finally in place it will surely affect hospitals, medical clinics, Medicare, and Medicaid. The chain reaction will impact many agencies.

A trend toward decentralization of federal government to state and local levels has been evident over the years. It is resulting in growing importance of state legislatures in societal issues.

3. Advocacy Groups

Advocacy and special interest groups are increasingly trying to create legislation, rulings, and attitudes that impact on agencies' missions. NPs themselves are sometimes actively engaged in lobbying as well as being affected by it.

4. Sociological Factors

This is a broad, complicated area encompassing the following:

- Demographics

- Education

- Occupation

- Income

- Health

- Crime

- Pollution

- Attitudes, values, customs, habits, policies

Here are some examples of the effect that sociological trends/developments can have on agencies.

- The rich-get-richer and the poor-get-poorer syndrome causes growing problems for agencies dealing with the destitute.

- The ever-shifting policies of private foundations in how and to whom they give their money away is a constant threat to agencies' fundraising programs.

- The use of robots in manufacturing is having major impact on employment which is affecting agencies dealing with the destitute and education.

- The large increase in single-parent families as a result of more divorces, separations, and children born out-of-wedlock can impact agencies for the destitute, mental health, and child care.

- By the year 2030, the entire baby boom generation — 77 million — will be senior citizens. Impact will be substantial on the family, nonprofit health agencies, for-profit providers, insurance companies, nursing homes, mental health agencies, social security, and whatever health care system will be in place at that time.

- The increase in the number of married women with children entering the workplace is affecting child care agencies as well as the host of problems that can result from lack of close parental supervision.

- The increase in pollution can have an effect on health agencies; measures to fight it will affect income.

- The upward trend of racism problems will continue to impact crime and education.

- The growing trend of partnerships — partnerships of NPs with government as well as partnerships with other NPs — means that agencies must be constantly on the lookout for affiliations and mergers.

5. Competition

Competition is seldom as important a factor with NPs as with FPs. This is generally true, but for some agencies competition can be formidable. For example:

- A small, inner-city private preparatory school in St. Louis experiences keen competition from all other private and public schools in the area, particularly those in the higher income suburban areas.

- A school for children with learning disabilities has no direct competition; however, it does have competition from a public special school district and a private school, both of whose missions are to provide education for disabled children. In addition, both private and public schools are trying to establish their own programs for children with special needs. For economic reasons, they tend to retain their own students rather than refer them to special schools where their needs might be better served.

- Agencies whose mission is to provide employment for the handicapped have lots of competition. They make products for sale to the government and often directly to consumers. Their competition is not only from private industry but also from other agencies that have the same mission and make the same products.

- Every agency is in competition with every other agencies in fundraising. Until quite recently, most agencies had an unplanned, unsophisticated approach to this activity. Now, most agencies have their own development director and often use a fund-raising professional to help them plan their approach.

So, whereas NPs do not usually have as severe competition as do FPs, they still have plenty. And it is frequently a factor in the external environment for creating a key issue.

6. Technology

All agencies have been affected by computers, iPads, iPhones, and robots for a host of analysis, communication, and operation activities.

Advances in DNA technology are having major impact upon health care and upon farming productivity of plants and animals.

MONITORING CHANGES IN THE EXTERNAL ENVIRONMENT

Sources of forecasts of the future are too numerous to provide an exhaustive list. They include books, periodicals, newspapers, TV programs, videotapes, and service organizations. But here are a few specifics for the economy, government, and society.

The Economy

Economic forecasts are liberally provided by the press and several services. *The Economist* and *Value Line* are major service providers for the U.S. and major world countries. *Currency Forecasters' Digest* concentrates on currency forecasts but also covers consensus economic forecasts for several countries. OECD (The Organization for Economic

Cooperation and Development) of Paris provides biannual forecasts of 24 countries; The International Monetary Fund of Washington D.C. provides biannual forecasts for seven major industrialized countries of the world — U.S., Canada, Japan, France, Germany, Italy, and the United Kingdom

Government

Keeping track and forecasting what new laws will be passed at the local, state, and federal levels — laws that can potentially impact on a given agency's operations — requires constant vigilance of the media and the publications designed to keep one current on legislation.

At the federal level is the *The Congressional Record Index.* This publication is designed to facilitate research on the status and history of legislation. Public bills and resolutions are listed, summarized, and indexed. The progress of bills through Congress is covered from introduction to final disposition.

At the state level, what is available will vary from state-to-state. The state of Missouri provides an example. *Legislative Report Service*, published by the Missouri Chamber of Commerce covers:

- Listing of Senate and House bills passed each session.

- Status of Senate and House bills.

- Hearing schedules.

- Committee Rosters.

- Bills' Analysis. (Only some bills, not all.)

In addition, the Missouri Chamber of Commerce publishes a weekly letter, *Legislation*. This covers major news items in the state legislature to keep organizations in- formed on issues that might affect their operations.

A 24-hour electronic service is also available; it shows calendars, bill listings, bill briefs, and status tables, all updated three times daily; it is handled through computer link.

Subscribers to the weekly service letter, *Legislation*, or the 24-hour bulletin board service, can utilize a customized bill tracking service for following specific legislation. Fees are based upon the number of bills requested to be tracked.

Finally, there are *District Files* which provide current information on all Missouri Senate and House Districts, updated annually. This publication includes:

- Personal profile on legislators.

- Analysis of their legislative activity.

- Voting history.

- Contribution history

- District demographic profile.

- Election history.

  Other states undoubtedly have similar services.

ANALYSIS TECHNIQUES

Impact of external developments is not easy to measure. Using sophisticated techniques to better judge the likelihood of occurrence of an event and its impact might sometimes be justified. Delphi, and Cross-Impact Analysis are two such techniques.

Delphi relies on obtaining a consensus of expert opinion. Great pains are taken to insure that the replies from the panel of experts are anonymous; this helps to eliminate behavioral problems that often occur when all members of the group are around a conference table; hence, replies to questions are usually handled by mail or FAX. After the first round of replies are received, the results are played back to the panel who are then given a chance to revise their original response should they choose to do so. The final step is an open around-the-table discussion of the estimates. The median of the estimates is the group decision.

Cross-Impact Analysis (CIA) is a technique for estimating the **combined impact** of all identified external environmental factors impacting on a project or key issue. A panel of "experts" is asked to assess the impact of each external factor on each key project factor using a scale of +10 (highly favorable impact) to -10 (highly negative impact). A computer set of calculations identifies the combined effect of all factors. For more information on **CIA**, John Wiley and Sons' book on the subject is recommended.

CONCLUSION

Being alert to what is happening to the external environment is a key factor to an agency's future. It is constantly changing. Some of the changes may provide new opportunities. Others may be threats.

Wang Laboratories, the United States automobile companies, and Sears Roebuck are examples in the business world where companies did not recognize soon enough what was happening, with dire results. The same thing can and does happen in the nonprofit world.

So what's the answer? Focus on developments that appear to have the potential for major impact. Constant coverage of the media is an important source for keeping current on what is happening. Be alert to articles and lectures on the subjects of interest and to opinion leaders' views on their trend and impact. Where more detailed information and analysis is needed, there is a host of special services that can be called upon, some of which are free, but many are costly.

For measuring the impact of external developments, there are several sophisticated techniques that can be used, such as, Delphi, Impact, and Cross Impact Analysis. In most situations these are too sophisticated and expensive to be used by nonprofits. Still, it is worthwhile to know that they exist on the chance that sometime an event might be sufficiently serious to justify their use.

CHAPTER FOUR

INTERNAL ENVIRONMENT

As mentioned earlier, the external environment and the internal environment are two major forces that impact on an institution's planning. Their analysis should uncover most of the key issues for which strategies and goals need to be developed. This chapter describes the nine areas that constitute the internal environment.

The external environment was defined as the outside forces that provide threats and opportunities to the institution's accomplishment of mission.

The internal environment is defined as:

The internal strengths and weaknesses of an agency that provide opportunities as well as create roadblocks to accomplishment of mission.

Analyzing strengths (S) and weaknesses (W) of the internal environment and the opportunities (O) and threats (T) of the external environment is a management technique commonly referred to as **SWOT Analysis**.

Major elements of the internal environment are:

1. Governance.

2. Physical facilities.

3. Organization.

4. Personnel/personnel practices.

5. Financial resources.

6. Proprietary know-how/skills

7. Management styles and idiosyncrasies

8. Brand.

Governance

Adequacy of bylaws and quality of the board of directors are often the most important internal environmental factors of NPs. Success or failure of an agency depends heavily on board quality. Because it is so important, the subject of governance is covered separately in Chapter Nine.

Physical Facilities

Physical facilities of NPs often suffer from not having been planned in advance of need. Too often agencies will make a physical facility change in the most expedient manner; they do not have a master plan of how space demands will grow; nor have they planned in advance how space will be provided as needs change.

Many years of little or no planning can result in a facilities nightmare: inefficient heating and cooling systems with utility expenses far beyond what they should be, inadequate parking area, poor departmental layout drastically reducing personnel efficiency. Sometimes the situation can become so bad that the only practical solution is to abandon present plant and build or buy another.

New or renovated physical facilities require new capital. Hence, financial planning for present and future physical facility needs is a necessary companion. Raising money for bricks and mortar is usually separated from the operating expense fundraising effort: contributors tend to look upon giving money for capital additions/alterations differently from that for operations.

The capital needed for new facilities must be determined and carefully evaluated as to whether the amount is realistically possible. A professional fundraiser may be needed to identify that. If it is not realistic, plans must be scaled back and/or extended in time.

If a new facility or renovation of the present one is needed, someone who has experience in the construction industry should be on the Board.

But requiring a completely new facility is extreme. Usually the need is less than that and sometimes conceivably a smaller facility might be indicated. In any case, it is important to look into the future five to ten years and decide if new or modified physical facilities will be needed and, if so, what and when.

Here is a checklist of questions which may be useful in evaluating the situation:

- Is the present facility well located to serve customers/clients?

- Are demographic trends such that sometime in the future, the present location will not be well suited to serve customers/clients?

- What is the long-term outlook of demand for your services/product? Will they grow or shrink?

- Could some alterations reduce utility costs; if so, would capital costs justify the savings?

- Can the new or renovated facilities be built in stages? If so, how?

- What is happening to the neighborhood where the facility is currently located? Is it a safe place for personnel? Will it be safe 5-10 years from now?

- What are long term projections for personnel needs and space requirements?

- Are there potential environmental problems in connection with the agency's operations or nearby operations of others?

- Is there a public relations problem with present location? Is the surrounding neighborhood generally supportive, or at least not opposed, to the agency's operations? Might there be a zoning problem if the agency tried to expand present facilities?

Organization

Organization can be an important factor in large agencies; not so important in small ones. It is mostly concerned with the effectiveness of internal communications from top to bottom. If the entity has only a handful of people, personnel policy has more to do with effectiveness of internal communications than organization structure. But if the entity is large with many employees and several departments, organization structure can be a major determinant of the quality of internal communications.

The book shelves are full of writings on organization principles and theory. It is not the intent of this book to reiterate all of these teachings. But we do wish to point out those principles that are particularly applicable to nonprofit agencies.

- Be sure that members of the organization understand all strategies and goals pertaining to their jobs.

- Recognize the theories on span of control: at the top level, no one person should supervise more than five or six other individuals if their work is complex and non-routine. If work is simple, routine, and repetitive, supervising 25 to 30 people is OK.

- Maintain short lines of communications. Keep the echelon layers to a minimum.

- Plan the evolution of your organization structure in advance of it becoming a critical issue. Drastic change in organization structure is disruptive. Gradual change is the way to go.

Personnel

Good quality does not just happen; it stems largely from the leadership of the entity and the personnel practices that it follows.

Neither is top quality personnel the whole answer. In addition to having highly skilled, intelligent, personable people, to use them productively requires a system of management that molds them into a team, motivates them, and fully uses their capabilities.

In both NPs and FPs, seldom are the capabilities of employees used to full advantage. Certainly it does not just happen; one has to work at it through systems of communications and training. Many consultants make fortunes selling their proprietary systems for accomplishing that objective.

Here is a checklist of questions that may help identify your strengths and weaknesses in this area:

- Do you have some staff and/or board people who have exceptional skills in certain areas? If so, are you fully utilizing these talents to help realize your mission and carry-out strategies?

- Do you have the reputation of being a fine place to work?

- Are salary levels and fringe benefits competitive?

- Do you have a high turnover of personnel? If so, do you know the causes?

- Do you have a system of communications whereby staff, board members, and clients feel that they have an opportunity to make known their thoughts, ideas, feelings about important issues, strategies, goals, and operations?

- What are the strengths and weaknesses of your chief executive officer?

- Do you have replacement plans for key personnel?

- Do you have training programs and lateral promotion plans to give the necessary training to key personnel and candidates for key positions?

- Do you have a system for setting individual goals that are tied into the NP's goals?

- Do you carry out appraisal interviews on a regular basis?

- Are all positions covered with job descriptions?

- Do you have a personnel manual?

Financial Resources

Financial resources are a major determinant of the extent to which strategies and goals can be pursued. There is little point in planning a new facility, or hiring new personnel, or expanding the scope of activities, if the amount of money to be raised for accomplishment is not realistic.

The financial situation of NPs run the full spectrum. Most NPs are in dire need of additional funds. Some are comfortable. A few have more financial resources than they need and are faced with trying to find new activities that can justify their existence. Whatever is the true situation is a key factor in establishing what pursuit of strategies is possible.

Here is a checklist to help you evaluate your agency's financial situation:

- Is the fundraising trend up, down, or static?

- Does the agency have any unrealized potential in fundraising?

- Do you have a satisfactory budgetary control system?

- Has the agency been able to live within its budget in most years?

- What is the debt situation? Does the agency have a credit rating that permits it to use bank loans at favorable interest rates?

- What is the ratio of current assets to current liabilities? This is known as the current ratio and should be, at least, about two-to-one.

- Have maintenance expenses and replacement schedules been at a level which keeps physical facilities in good shape and eliminates the danger of a catastrophic fire?

- Is there any danger of losing not-for-profit status?

Proprietary Skills

Proprietary know-how/skill can be a tremendous asset. An example is an agency that hired a development director who turned out to have unique skill in this area. Her success opened up a whole new horizon for this agency to the extent that it decided to raise money for other causes and change its mission.

Management Prejudices

Learn the orientations and prejudices of your CEO so time won't be wasted in pursuing projects that have little chance of acceptance.

A host of factors can cause change in top management attitudes: personal problems; changes in the economic climate; lame duck situations if the CEO is close to retirement; past negative experiences.

Brand

The word "brand" historically has referred to product brands. No longer – now the word refers to people and organizations as well as products. If you are looking for a job, for instance, you might now be asked for your "brand" – a much broader description of you and your experience than can be found in your resume.

Creating a brand for an NP is covered in a book published in 2014: "The Brand Idea – Managing Nonprofit Brands with Integrity, Democracy, and Affinity" by Nathalie Laidler-Kylander and Julia Shepard Stenzel. Interviews with over 70 NP organizations explore in detail how NPs are pursuing ways of using their brands

STRENGTHS/WEAKNESSES ANALYSIS

The final result of all this introspection should be documentation of the organization's strengths and weaknesses. Listing them under these two headings helps to crystallize key issues.

Here is an example taken from a community service organization for families and individuals under stress; services include day care, education, recreation, counseling, vocational training, work placement, and direct relief.

Strengths

- Excellent leadership by the Executive Director.

- Dedicated and strongly motivated staff.

- Deep involvement by staff in community organizations giving them a grass-roots feel of problems in the community.

- Excellent education program in day care.

- Volunteers, dedicated and excellent quality.

- Strong Board of Directors.

- Excellent physical facilities, debt free.

Weaknesses

- Unrealized potential in fundraising; no development director; most fundraising carried out and directed by Executive Director.

- Shortage of staff to meet current demand.

- Improvements needed in staff training programs.

- Volunteers do not receive adequate orientation because of staff shortage.

- Not enough volunteers; existing ones are overworked.

- Poor attendance at Board and committee meetings.

- Current bylaws call for prospective Board members to have certain community and church affiliations This rules out availability of some prospects who otherwise would be desirable candidates.

- Additional plant is needed for growth of current programs.

- Too many exits/entrances to building create security problem.

- Parking facilities are inadequate.

From this analysis, it was agreed that the key issues were:

- Fundraising.

- Need to change bylaws to eliminate special requirements for prospective board members.

- Need to improve personnel department.

- Need for a long range plan for physical facilities.

CONCLUSION

Analysis of the internal environment in many ways is more difficult than analysis of the external environment. The factors tend to be more subtle and often difficult to state openly, particularly if they involve personalities and idiosyncrasies of staff or board members.

Use of consultants can often be the best route to presenting conclusions of these sensitive areas to top level staff and board members. We have many times seen board situations so bad that the advice was "have everyone on the present board resign and start over again." Or, "your biggest problem is the executive director; get rid of him/her." An outsider can get away with making such drastic recommendations, for an insider it is difficult.

CHAPTER FIVE

KEY ISSUES

At this juncture, the present **situation** of the agency has been described; its **mission** has been stated; the important features of the **internal and external environments** that may have significant impact on the agency have been identified. The next step is decision on **key issues**.

Key Issues are problems and/or opportunities that potentially could have major impact on the agency – not a laundry-list of all or most of the problems/opportunities of the agency. They usually number a half-dozen or less.

Effective selection of key issues requires: solid analysis of the present situation, an excellent statement of mission, realistic identification of the external and internal environments; and good judgment on their interpretation.

Here is a real-life case history to demonstrate the process.

Fischer School (fictitious name) is a coeducational, private, college-preparatory school covering grades seven through twelve. It was launched fifteen years ago for the purpose of providing quality middle school education to deserving students who might not ordinarily be able to afford private schooling. The founders were two individuals who had previously taught in both public and private schools.

Initial enrollment was 50 students. After ten years, enrollment had reached 200 students. Then within three years, enrollment dropped to 125. Reasons for the decrease were believed to be:

1. Demographics: fewer children of eligible age.

2. Increased competition, largely from busing blacks into the excellent school systems of the city's suburbs.

3. Some negative reactions to a temporary lowering of entrance requirements which overcrowded the school and let in some undesirables.

The enrollment drop caused such a financial bind that the school considered discontinuing operations. At this point the school sought the help of consultants to help lead the way out of the financial crisis and develop a long range plan.

The school's **Mission** read as follows:

Fischer School is a coed college preparatory institution where students mature and develop socially and academically through a rich tradition of study and diverse experiences.

The college preparatory curriculum at Fischer is a challenging one that exists in a humanistic atmosphere in which students strive to learn because they enjoy it, not because they fear failure. To that end, Fischer seeks to create an atmosphere of constructive competition in which students are encouraged to "own" their successes, and to take pride in their growth and development, while recognizing the sensibilities of their fellow students.

Fischer is dedicated to serving a cross section of the community, including all races and all economic strata. Because Fischer believes that learning can take place both in and outside the classroom, students at Fischer take numerous field trips.

The rapport between students and faculty at Fischer is exceptionally good, and teachers at Fischer are not afraid to be in a situation in which they come to command respect rather than demand it.

The college preparatory curriculum at Fischer is a challenging one, but it is not so demanding that it becomes unrealistic for students to meet their responsibilities in an honest and self-reliant fashion. Competition among students is discouraged; rather students are encouraged to "own" their own successes and take pride in their growth and development.

The major factors in the **External Environment** were:

Threats

1. Demographics were unfavorable: fewer children of eligible age in the area.

2. Through a desegregation plan, most blacks who want a better education than they can receive in the city's public schools opt for being bused to the suburbs. There is no offsetting migration of white students from suburban schools to city schools.

3. Few whites are left in the city's public schools. Those that are left tend to choose parochial schools.

4. Likelihood of an economic recession within the next two years.

Opportunities

1. Problems in the educational system of a nearby area which is not included in the desegregation plan. Most families in this area can afford private school tuition.

2. Another, even larger nearby area, but with lower per capita income than the one above, has poor public education facilities and is believed to have pent-up-demand for an independent, non-sectarian private school.

3. No foreseeable increase in competition from private schools in suburban areas.

4. Low inflation — two to three percent over the next five years.

The **Internal Environment** was identified as follows:

Strengths

1. Excellent faculty with strong allegiance to school's teaching principles and mission. Many teachers choose this school over the more prestigious suburban private schools.

2. High quality of student body. Many of the students are accepted in Ivy League schools.

3. Strong parent involvement in some activities.

4. Favorable location of physical facilities relative to its market.

5. Favorable economics of physical facilities. Low overhead.

6. Free use of nearby public recreation/athletic facilities.

7. Tuition level $2,000 to $3,000 below other independent private schools.

Weaknesses

1. Low student enrollment. A minimum of 150 is needed for financial stability.

2. Salaries and benefits for faculty not at levels of other independent private schools.

3. Low parent involvement in many activities.

4. Insufficient financial reserves. Inadequate fundraising.

5. Leased facilities present a danger to remaining at present location.

6. No gymnasium.

7. The appearance of physical facilities, both outside and inside, is not up to standards of most other independent private schools with whom the school is in competition.

8. Population trend is away from the city to the north. The school may experience a declining market.

9. The name of the school and its fine attributes are not well known in the community.

The above analysis of the external and internal environment of the school resulted in the following list of **Key Issues:**

1. Recruitment

How to ensure enrollment of at least 150 students each year? The school cannot be as selective in admissions as it would like with 60 to 80 applicants per year. A larger number of applicants is needed. More applicants would mean that more academically qualified prospects would be full-paying students.

2. Development

How to improve fundraising? The current development effort is weak. Parent giving has averaged only $125 per family; less than 70% of families give anything; outside giving totals less than $30,000 per year.

3. Physical Facilities

How to improve the quality of the school's physical facility? The structure was initially a grocery store. The school does not have a gym and both the library and assembly rooms are limited in size. The facility is leased from a landlord who is having financial problems. The present rent does not generate any profit for the landlord; the school's lease could therefore be a target for higher rent payment. The city's population is moving north; the school may therefore experience a declining market.

4. Staff Salaries

The current median salary of the school's faculty is about 10% less than the salary levels of its private school competition and about 20% less than that of its public school counterparts. To retain and attract quality teachers, the school must commit itself to a policy of predictable and significant pay increases.

5. Financial Stability

The school has no significant financial reserves. Its assets are limited; they include no physical facilities. There is little protection against temporary hardship.

CONCLUSION

Selection of key issues is the crux of the planning process. Some are completely obvious. But often they are subtle, not easily identified. And sometimes they are so political that they are difficult to bring out into the open; this is particularly true when a key issue is concerned with competency of staff and/ or governing board.

Thoughtful development of the agency's current situation and mission combined with thorough analysis of its external threats and opportunities and its internal strengths and weaknesses should uncover most, if not all, of the key issues.

Staff and perhaps other stakeholders should be exposed to a planning committee's tentative conclusions and the background information that lead up to these conclusions. Taking the time for this step is not only good for public and staff relations, but also may uncover other key issues that were missed.

CHAPTER SIX

STRATEGIES AND GOALS

A strategy is the best choice of alternatives for dealing with a key issue; goals are the expected results of implementing that strategy.

The business world is full of right and wrong strategy decisions. Coca-Cola in 1985 was losing market share to Pepsi-Cola. After $4 millions of research, the company announced in April, 1985, that it was going to change its formula; this was the strategy to recapture market share. Media later described it as "The Marketing Blunder of the Century"[1]. Sales plummeted. On July 10, 1985, the company returned to the old formula under the name, "Coca-Cola Classic."

---

[1]"For God, Country and Coca Cola," Mark Pendergrast, Page 354. Macmillan Publishing Company, 1993.

Wang Laboratories' decision in the 1970's to leave the highly competitive calculators business and switch to computer-based integrated information processing systems met with fabulous success — for a while. Then in the early 1990's, Wang went into bankruptcy for not keeping up with the times in this rapidly changing industry.

The nonprofit world does not have as many dramatic examples but they are just as common. The Fischer School, mentioned in Chapter Five, almost went out of existence because of a bad strategic decision to expand enrollment by lowering entrance requirements.

Analysis and *Alternatives* are the tools for making decisions on strategies.

Analysis

Thorough analysis of one's situation is essential. In the for-profit business world, companies often spend thousands of man-hours and dollars using analytical techniques that they think will help point the way to key issues and strategies and goals. Over 30 such techniques have been identified.[2] They include such disciplines as Product Life Cycle Analysis, Experience Curves, Product Portfolio Analysis, Futures Studies, Multiple Scenarios, and many others.

Most of these 30 are too oriented to FPs to be of interest to NPs. But a few are applicable. We have already mentioned **SWOT Analysis** in Chapter Four.

Benchmarking[3] is another. Benchmarking is the process of studying in depth the operations of one's strongest competitors. It is a structured and thorough approach to examine what the most successful agencies are doing, how they do it, and then deciding how one might copy them.

---

[2]James L. Webster, William E. Reif, Jeffrey S. Bracker, "The Manager's Guide to Strategic Planning Tools and Techniques." *Planning Review*, November/December, 1989, Page 4.

[3]"Strategic Benchmarking: How to Pick the Right Target," *Planning Review*, January/February, 1993.

The first step is deciding which operations should be analyzed and what areas provide the best opportunities for improvement: fundraising, public relations, governance, planning, etc. Once this decision has been made, the next step is to study in detail how the most successful agencies manage these areas.

One problem with this technique, unique to NPs, is that an agency will frequently have little or no direct competition. But even if an agency is not offering the same service, it may have superior performance in some areas that are applicable to other agencies – fundraising, for example. Some agencies are very effective fund raisers; how they do it can be studied and copied to great advantage. Governance is another.

One aspect of **Zero-Base Budgeting** can also be a useful technique for NPs. Zero-Base Budgeting is the process of developing a budget without reference to what has gone on before. The aspect that is particularly useful is the setting of priorities by asking the question: if the agency can carry out one program, which will it be. If two programs, which will they be. And so on until the agency reaches its limit on resources to carry out any more programs.

Alternatives

Too often agencies will decide on a single strategy for solving a key issue without considering other possibilities. They select the obvious, but sometimes the obvious is not the best. An example is the agency that decided to build new facilities to take care of its need for more space; if it had considered already existing facilities that could be

purchased and modified, the cost of expanded space would have been significantly reduced.

An agency providing employment to the handicapped had experienced significant decrease in demand for its products because the U.S. government had sharply reduced purchases because of budgetary pressures.

The alternatives were: (1) try to sell directly to private consumers; (2) expand sales to the government by broadening its line of products; (3) try to do both.

The agency selected alternative (3). Direct sales to the private consumer turned out to be a dismal failure; the agency did not have the expertise or financial resources to handle this new activity. Expanding its product base to the government, on the other hand, was highly successful; this is where it had years of experience with lots of know-how.

CHAPTER SEVEN

FINANCIAL FORECASTS

In the early years of planning, making financial forecasts for budgetary purposes was the **only** planning carried out. Today budgeting is relatively insignificant compared to the total process of strategic planning.

BUDGETING

Budgeting is a universal practice of both NPs and FPs. It is a part of the planning process. In fact, budgeting gave birth to long range planning; it was practiced first and long range planning followed. That is why many planning departments were originally part of the Finance Department of corporations.

The budget is the expected financial results of the first year of a strategic plan. The process typically begins a few months before the end of the fiscal year to cover the year ahead. The target is usually to have an approved budget before year end. Often, however, finalization is not accomplished until one or two months into the year covered by the budget. The subject is well documented by other books. This chapter points out those aspects of the subject that are most important for NP planning.

Styles of Budgeting

Three basic styles of carrying out the budgeting process are; (1) bottom-up, (2) top-down; and (3) zero-base budgeting (ZBB), mentioned in Chapter Six.

Bottom-up budgeting is practiced in larger agencies which have several departments/ divisions. The first step is to provide guidelines to managers who are responsible for preparing budgets for their activities. These guidelines identify approved programs; list basic assumptions, such as, the economic climate; provide format to be followed; and indicate content to be covered. All of the managers' figures, when developed, are consolidated into an entity total. At this point it may be necessary to go back to managers for revisions if totals seem unrealistic.

Top-down budgets are prepared by top-level staffs for the total agency's operations. These would be for the smaller agencies that are not departmentalized. But even here, the top-level staff people often consult lower echelons who have some responsibility for implementing approved programs.

Zero-Base Budgeting (ZBB)

Preparation of budgets are usually carried out on an incremental basis. That is, the amounts spent for line-items or programs during the current fiscal year are increased or decreased for the next year. ZBB starts from a zero base as if all programs had never before existed and must be justified all over again in competition with all other programs.

In contrast to conventional budgeting, ZBB assumes the posture that a program does not necessarily continue next year just because it was funded the past year. Projects that contribute little to an agency's mission are assigned a low priority; in competition with other programs they may be reduced or eliminated. It's a valuable prioritization concept.

The one disadvantage of ZBB is that it makes the budgeting process much more detailed and complex. For this reason, seldom do organizations go through the process every year.

Financial forecasts try to identify what the bottom-line results will be if the strategies are successfully executed. They will be inaccurate; make them anyway; they will become the base for improving their accuracy with the passage of time and they may become a necessity if they will be needed for financing needs of the organization.

Many assumptions will be required in making the forecasts:

- Forecast of the economy including inflation.
- The time factor of success in carrying out strategies
- The cost of carrying out strategies
- Income, if any, from carrying out strategies

From the above, develop 1-5 year balance sheets and income statements; how far out and how much detail will depend upon circumstances. For instance, if one is looking for a bank loan more detail is needed: the financial forecasts will probably have to be by months for the first year and by quarters for succeeding years. This enables the bank to track closely the safety of getting its loan repaid.

Carefully document the assumptions. Some will not happen as predicted. Their documentation will facilitate correcting forecasted figures as some become evident that they are wrong.

CHAPTER EIGHT

PLANNING CONTROL

The greatest value of strategic planning is often viewed as simply going through the process — not the long range plan itself. This is certainly true if the agency in question files the document away after it is completed and seldom, if ever, looks at it again. This should not happen, but often does. The following are needed to insure that the plan is used:

- Watchdog control

- Action Programs

- Annual Reviews

WATCHDOG CONTROL

Major responsibility for seeing that a long range plan is used must be that of the chief executive officer (CEO) of the agency. If the head of an agency does not assume this role, nothing will happen. But the burden can be lightened by appointing someone on the Board of Directors to be chairman of a long range planning committee

This person should play a major role in developing the long range plan, be constantly alert to necessary revisions, and monitor its implementation.

The entire Board of Directors should be watchdogs. They should be completely knowledgeable of what is said in the written plan, constantly probe the extent to which it is being implemented, and keep a focus on critical issues.

Staff must also be committed to ensuring that an approved plan is implemented. Board members have a limit on how much time they can spend on an agency's plans and problems. The major responsibility for implementing strategies lies with staff.

Interface between staff and board members is a necessary ingredient for both groups to meet their respective responsibilities. Some institutions do this by having board members attend a staff/management conference to review forward plans. Others have staff presentations at board meetings.

ACTION PROGRAMS

Action programs identify in detail who is going to do what/when in fulfilling a strategy; they pin responsibility on individuals for seeing that the job gets done.

In this connection some mention should be made of PERT — Program Evaluation and Review Technique; it's a planning tool for *visually* identifying all of the actions that must be taken to arrive at the end result of a complex program.

PERT's use can only be justified in complicated situations where many actions are required to achieve an end result and where visual communication of the plan is desirable.

It identifies all of the actions that must be taken plus time estimates, cost estimates, and probabilities of accuracy - all placed in a computer so that the final result can be regurgitated as various elements of the plan require adjustment.

ANNUAL REVIEW

The Board chair, chairman of the planning committee, and the CEO should work together in instigating an annual review to establish progress on key issues and determine if revisions should be made in any/all aspects of the plan. Here are some of the questions they should ask:

1. Is the mission statement out-of-date? Does it need revision?

2. Have the external and internal environments changed sufficiently to require revisions in the current plan?

3. Are there any problems with present by-laws? Should they be revised?

4. Is the Board properly balanced in terms of expertise and commitment?

5. Are priorities on programs still valid? What does the cost/benefit picture look like for present programs? Should any programs be dropped?

6. Should any new programs be considered in view of anticipated changes in the external and internal environments?

7. Should stakeholders be surveyed to determine their satisfaction with delivery of services and to solicit their suggestions for improvement?

8. Is the development program compatible with current and future financial needs? Are income and expenditure projections realistic?

9. Is the development director doing a good job? What are his/her strengths and weaknesses. Can the weaknesses be supported with more help from the Board and/or from a professional fund raiser?

10. Is reporting on performance adequate to identify successes and failures so that, if necessary, corrective actions can be taken?

CHAPTER NINE

GOVERNANCE

A strong, dedicated Board and high quality leadership of the Board Chair and the salaried CEO are the most important ingredients for successful nonprofits organizations.

Sometimes having a Board of Directors at all is questioned; why not just elect one person to run the operation? Such a setup can work well as long as that one person is still alive and remains dedicated and active. But time takes its toll — particularly when leadership rolls are dependent on volunteers. That is why for-profit corporations and nonprofits have universally adopted the Board of Directors style of governance. It is the most efficient system thus far invented for providing good governance.

Governance is a persistent problem with NPs. Poorly conceived bylaws and ungraceful aging are most often the causes. What was once a fine board often degenerates over time; some board members may have stagnated having remained on the board too long; the agency's needs of the board may have changed. This chapter examines these problems and suggests how to avoid them.

BYLAWS

Bylaws problems stem from two principal sources: (1) they were badly conceived from the beginning; (2) they have become out-of-date and need to be revised to reflect the up-to-date needs of the organization and changes in the external environment. Problems are often a combination of both.

Here is a list of **Do's** and **Don'ts**

Do's

1. Provide for rotation of board members. Any board member, no matter how good he/she was initially, will tend to become stale and ineffective if allowed to stay too long. Require reelection every three or four years; three is most common.

2. Limit the number of times a person can be reelected; twice is a frequent choice with the opportunity to be elected again after being off the board for one year. This provides for eliminating "deadwood" without embarrassment.

3. Elect one-third of the board members every year so that there will not be a large influx of new members in any one year and so that there will always be a "seasoned" group of individuals on the board.

4. Provide for revision of bylaws through two-thirds vote of the board members. This can be done in two ways: either by a two-thirds vote of a quorum at a board meeting or two-thirds vote of the total board with the votes of non-present members obtained by phone. We lean toward the latter if the board is strong and dedicated with little or no deadwood in its make-up.

5. Provide for a well-balanced board. There should be expertise in planning, finance, law, and "contacts" for fundraising purposes. Other kinds of expertise will depend upon the nature of the agency. For instance, if it is an organization dedicated to helping handicapped children (mentally and/or physically), a child psychologist on the board might be desirable.

Don'ts

1. Don't put restrictions on persons to qualify for board membership. Often when agencies are initially created, it seems like a good idea to require that all or a large proportion of the board members come from the universe that it serves. For instance, an agency to help people with learning disabilities required that some or all board members be made up of parents who have children with learning disability problems. Another agency required boards members to serve on its advisory board for a minimum period before becoming eligible to be a board member.

Such restrictions simply create roadblocks to attracting individuals on a board that might be most qualified. If, for instance, the board needs a lawyer, whether or not the most desirable legal person has children with disabilities may be completely irrelevant. This does not mean that a board should be devoid of individuals from the service universe, but it should not be a requirement. Furthermore, such individuals should be kept to small numbers because they tend to be unable to be dispassionate and objective.

The advisory board requirement prior to eligibility on the governing board has two negatives: (1) it makes the advisory board members feel as though they are second-class citizens; (2) the best prospects for new board members may be unwilling to serve a second-class citizenship position before qualifying for board membership.

2. Don't have too many persons qualified to attend board meetings. Twenty board members should be a maximum for large agencies; twelve, for smaller ones. If you have an advisory board, consider carefully whether you want them to attend boards meetings or to meet separately. If they are invited to attend regular board meetings, it is awkward to exclude them from voting on board matters or to excuse them from the meeting when the time has

come for voting on such matters. Also, too many people around the table slows up the decision-making process.

THE BOARD

An invitation to be on a nonprofit board, is seldom received with an understanding of entailed responsibilities unless the individual has been on other boards and received some training. Acceptance entails both financial and time commitment.

Major Responsibilities

In very general terms, a board member's responsibility is one of auditing rather than running programs. It should be recognized, however, that there is a difference between *the board* and *board members*. Although it might be inappropriate, for instance, that *the board* become involved in running programs of the agency, individual *board members* might have expertise that suggests their participation in running some aspects of programs.

Major responsibility is to make certain that the agency is viable both in terms of its mission and in the quality of its CEO.

An agency's mission tends to be long term. But that does not mean that it should never change. With time, it may become out-of-date and require fine tuning or major redefinition. It is the boards responsibility to be alert to such aging process and make timely changes as needed.

The board selects the CEO; it is also responsible for evaluating his/her performance, for providing adequate compensation, and for maintaining a supportive environment. Close relationship between the board and the CEO with mutual respect for each other is important.

Ensuring that the agency has adequate financial resources is high on the list of board responsibility. The board member should personally provide a substantial annual gift. Equally important is volunteer support to the fundraising effort in providing contacts to potential givers and writing personal longhand messages on letters of solicitation to people he/she knows. Finally, the board is responsible for seeing that the fundraising effort is properly organized. This usually means hiring a part-time or full-time development director sometimes supported by a fund-raiser consultant.

In the planning area, the board's responsibility is to audit and approve rather than do the planning. Some board members, however, may be on the planning committee; then, they do become involved in the planning process.

The board should also ensure that the planning process is carried out. If the agency does not have a strategic plan, it should take whatever action is necessary to initiate the process. If too much time has gone by since the last plan was written or revised, it should instigate an update of the present plan.

Approving, and auditing programs is the final major responsibility of the board. The agency's staff will normally be the principal driving force in suggesting and carrying out programs. Even though board members do not have responsibility for carrying out programs they can be very helpful in suggesting programs.

Other responsibilities of the board include: critique and approve the annual budget; monitor performance versus the budget throughout the year and recommend corrective action where variation from budget is substantial; protect and enhance the agency's public image; constantly be alert to opportunities for improving the quality of board membership.

Board Make-Up

Certain kinds of expertise are needed on boards. Legal is one; a lawyer who can advise the board on legal matters. Not only can such a person help an agency stay clear of legal problems, but also avoid the expense of a lawyer's fee every time a legal question arises.

A person with strong background in finance and controllership is another: someone who can help design the control reports needed for financial control of the operation; who can advise the agency on how to get the best return on excess cash; watch over the budgetary control system; and make sure that the books are audited each year. The latter can be a particularly important factor in money-raising; most foundations will not consider giving money to an agency unless an annual audit is standard practice.

Other useful expertise on boards include someone who has a strong background in strategic planning and experience in fundraising. If the agency has a development director, presumably this person would have the experience needed and be an ex-officio member of the board.

Board Organization

The board chairman is normally elected by the board. He/she should never be the CEO.

All boards should have committees — some standing committees, some ad hoc. None of these committees need be comprised solely of board members; volunteers and staff can be on them as well. Their purpose is to study major issues in depth and recommend their resolution to the board or to continuously watch over important areas, such as, planning, finance, etc. The principle behind this approach is that it provides greater in-depth study of the areas covered and saves time. In other words, it gets the job done better and faster than trying to involve the entire board in the process.

The number of committees should be kept to a minimum. Too many cause dilution of board members' responsibilities. All board committees should be kept active; inactive ones should be eliminated. The following five are most common:

Executive Committee

Long Range Planning

Finance

Operations

Fundraising and public relations

An Executive Committee to handle important matters between board meetings is often an expedient necessity. Such a committee is often comprised of the board chair, the CEO, and chairpersons of board committees. About one-third the size of the board is usually about right unless the board is abnormally large (over 20). It should meet only when time constraints make it necessary. The Executive Committee becoming so powerful that it usurps board responsibility is a danger to avoid.

The Long Range Planning Committee is responsible for ensuring that a long range plan is in existence and kept up-to-date. The committee should be chaired by the chairperson of the long range planning committee of the board. The CEO and the chief financial officer should definitely be members. Others might be the board chair, development director, or any other board or staff members who have demonstrated strong interest, good judgment, and conceptual thinking capability.

The Finance Committee, chaired by the Treasurer, is responsible for overseeing the finances of the agency and designing a financial reporting system that provides easily analyzed, timely reports for review by board members.

The Operations Committee is key to good governance. This committee oversees the management and effectiveness of programs to help ensure that they are accomplishing their goals and that such goals are still valid. But watch out! Do not let its members become involved in running programs rather than just overseeing them.

The Fund Raising/Public Relations Committee's responsibility is to oversee and assist wherever possible in fund raising and public relations activities. This includes being alert to opportunities for good publicity. The chair of this activity should have broad contacts among potential givers and the media; also have some knowledge/experience in the techniques of press releases. Responsibilities include: overseeing the preparation and execution of the annual fundraising plan; participating in its execution; evaluating effectiveness in both development and obtaining favorable publicity.

A Nominating Committee for nominating board members and officers should be ad-hoc. It is appointed by the board chair and usually comprised of individuals who have had lots of experience with the agency and who are no longer themselves potential candidates, such as, past officers.

Other committees will depend upon the nature of the agency. For instance if it is an association, a Membership Committee might be in order; if the agency has substantial physical property to look after, a Building and Grounds Committee might be needed.

Board Meetings

Who chairs the board is of vital importance to its effectiveness. Attending board meetings should be fun. But so often they become a drudgery and a frustrating experience, all because the chairperson is inept at conducting a meeting. Loss of good board members can result.

The extent to which formal parliamentary procedure is used must be weighed carefully. Determining factors are size and compatibility of board members. If the board is small — say, 12 members or less — and there are no, or very few, members who have a tendency to talk too much, and all show mutual respect and courtesy toward each other, then informal procedure is the way to go. Even so, the chairperson should know well Robert's Rules of Order and tell the board they will be used whenever appropriate. Some agencies will want to state in their bylaws that Robert's Rules of Order will be used in conducting meetings. We personally do not think that this is necessary unless it is a very large agency with a large board.

Much has been written on techniques for conducting meetings. But no amount of reading or attending seminars on the subject can provide the "feel" of the chairperson for when to utilize prerogatives of the chair and when to allow discussion to continue freely. It requires thorough understanding of each individual around the table and astute diplomacy.

We feel that there are a few aspects to running meetings that are particularly important:

1. Have an agenda for all meetings and stick to it. The agenda should be available to members at least a day before the meeting. As a first order of business, ask for approval of the agenda, as presented. If suggestions are made for deletions or additions, let the board vote on whether the changes should be made.

2. Start the meeting on time. A new chairperson will almost always discover that several board members will not yet have arrived at the designated starting time. Begin the meeting anyway. They will soon learn that they either arrive on time or miss the early part of meetings. It is only fair to the others who *do* arrive on time.

3. State in your bylaws what constitutes a quorum. It is frustrating for board members to arrive at a meeting and discover that there are not enough members present to hold the meeting. For that reason, we are in favor of the bylaws stating that a quorum is "whoever shows up **for a properly called general meeting.**"

4. Keep discussion on the subject. If it wanders onto another subject already on the agenda, state that it will be discussed when that part of the agenda is reached. If the subject is not on the agenda for the current meeting, suggest that it be placed on the agenda for a future meeting.

5. When a motion is made, make sure that it is seconded. If not, it dies without discussion. If it is seconded, put it in writing if there is *any* chance that its length and complicity might result in it being misconstrued by some board members; read it before discussion begins.

6. Keep order. Insist that attendees be recognized by the chair before speaking unless the small size of the group obviates the necessity of such a formality.

7. Distribute reports to be discussed at board meetings at least a day before the scheduled meeting. It is unrealistic to expect board members to effectively react to a written report unless they have had a chance to read the report before the meeting, not at the meeting.

8. Duration of meetings should be held to two hours with an absolute time limit of three hours; have recesses, every ninety minutes.

Advisory Councils

Advisory groups are becoming ever more popular with nonprofits. They go by various names; we prefer "council." It denotes a certain element of prestige; concurrently it does not provide any connotation of decision-making authority.

Sometimes agencies will create an ad-hoc advisory group to deal with a specific, current pressing issue. Here we are principally concerned with the permanent variety, not ad-hoc groups.

Some advisory councils are well conceived. Many are not. If properly structured, they can be of real value. If not, they can be a problem.

What are the key factors? Before forming an advisory council, consider very carefully what you expect it to do for you, how it will operate, and how it will be constituted. Here are some key factors that can contribute to their success.

1. Define in writing why you want an advisory council and specifically what its role will be. After it has been created, review the stated purpose at least annually to ensure that it is still valid.

2. Place a limitation on size; define the kinds of people that should comprise its membership; provide for rotation to avoid development of deadwood.

3. Be sure the CEO looks upon the advisory council as being highly worthwhile and is willing to spend the time to make it work.

4. Identify its relationship to the board, how it will interact with the Board.

5. Try to create an image that will cause people to feel that it would be a distinct honor to be invited to membership. One way to do this is to have a highly prestigious person as chair; fill out membership with others who are recognized as being outstanding citizens.

6. Have a written job description for council members.

Advisory councils are often created to enhance fundraising capability by inviting people to serve on it who are potentially large contributors and/or can open the door to large contributors. This is dangerous if this is the *principal* reason for creating an advisory council. It may weaken the rightful role of the board in fundraising. A better approach would be to enhance the fundraising capability by expanding or reconstituting the board than creating an advisory group for that purpose.

On the other hand, if the advisory council performs many other important roles, there is nothing wrong with asking it to *assist* the board in fundraising as long as it does not usurp a major part of the board's responsibility in this regard. If you need a home for big donors, call it a "special friends" group, not an advisory council.

The word "advisory" should mean just that. Authority should be limited to giving advice and counsel to the governing board, the CEO, or other staff members.

Membership should be open to anyone with unique experience and capability for providing helpful advice toward the agency's operations — like the child psychologist for an agency that exists to help the early education of mentally and/or physically handicapped children.

It is not recommended that advisory councils be used as a training ground for board members. It may happen that way in some instances. But if board members must serve a term on an advisory council before they become board members, as pointed out earlier, it may be a deterrent to obtaining the best board candidates.

How to Conduct a Board Survey

Governance problems often surface as a major issue when consultants are called in to help an agency initiate a long range planning process. Sometimes the problems will be so great that there is little point in initiating the process until the governance problems have been solved first. How does one go about identifying the major problems and arriving at their solution? A personal interview survey is usually the answer.

A consultant is the best one to conduct such a survey. Being an outsider, the interviewee will tend to be more open and have more faith that the information communicated will be held confidential than if conducted by an insider.

Those that should be interviewed are: the CEO, the board chairperson, other officers, and other board members. Other possibilities are past officers and past board members. Sometimes staff personnel might be considered.. Members of an advisory group should be considered, if one exists.

How many interviews should be carried out will depend upon the agency. Typically, as interviews are conducted, the same pattern of replies begin to emerge. At this point, the process can be stopped.

Here is a list of questions that, as appropriate, might be asked:

- How long have you been in your present status with the agency?

- What is your area of expertise?

- What do you think are the major strengths and weaknesses of the agency and specifically of the board?

- In your opinion, do the bylaws have any problems?

- Do board members adhere to the bylaws or do they tend to frequently disregard them?

- Does the agency have a strong, open-minded, creative, participatory board dedicated to pursuing the agency's goals?

- Are board members compatible with each other or is there open friction between some members?

- What do you understand to be your role in the affairs of the agency?

- If you are a board committee chairperson, what do you consider to be your assignment and responsibilities in that role?

- If you are the treasurer, who signs checks? How is surplus reinvested? What are the trends of costs and income? What is the overall financial health of the agency?

- What is the quality of the relationship between the board and staff? (Try to identify any conflicts.)

- Has the board clearly identified and communicated the agency's goals?

- Has the agency a strong, creative, dedicated staff?

- Does the board have any deficiencies in some important areas of expertise? What are they?

- Is there a training program for board members? Is it worthwhile?

- Does the agency have a long range planning document? Is it useful?

- In the area of fundraising, are you involved in the effort? How? Have you been personally asked to make a contribution?

- In your opinion, is the fundraising effort well administered? How is it organized?

- Does the agency have an adequate community relations program?

- Are internal communications adequate?

- What is the quality of leadership of the CEO and board chairperson?

- Does the agency have an effective training program for staff and volunteers to increase productivity and job satisfaction

- How would you rate the quality of board members? Is there any deadwood on the board? Do the bylaws provide for rotation?

- Are physical facilities adequate?

- Has the advisory council (if one exists) been worthwhile? What has it accomplished?

- What do you consider to be the key issues of the agency?